IN THE HOUSE OF LADDERS

for Ann

your eyes hold the
warm quiet dark
of sleeping books
waiting to be read

Bill Lewis

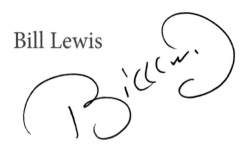

Billie.

IN THE HOUSE OF LADDERS

Poems

*To Maz
thanks for
your lovely
voice*

Greenheart Press

First published by Greenheart Press in 2012
Greenheart Press is an imprint of WOW Kent magazine
www.wowkent.co.uk

Typesetting by A Stone's Throw Design
Produced by The Choir Press

A CIP record for this book
is available from the British Library

ISBN 978-0-9571829-0-5

CONTENTS

All images are by the author

Preface

William Edward Lewis was born in the early Fifties in the village of Barming, near Maidstone. The world was in recovery from the war and Barming was then a small, rural place. An only child, he has very little collective memory about his family, either imparted or gathered after the facts.

"Someone once asked me why my stories are so strange and I said 'because both my parents are fictitious'. As soon as I said that I realized it was true, because I couldn't rely on anything they told me, or told each other."

The few facts Lewis does possess paint a fascinating picture. His father was a farm labourer, significantly older than Lewis's mother ("He was the same age as my friends' grandparents"). He spoke Romany, had an olive skin and a violent aversion to having his picture taken. Lewis remembers him pinning a hapless seaside photographer against a wall in Folkestone for attempting to take a snap and, years later, he attacked Lewis himself for the same.

Also working class, his mother appears to have been even more elusive than his father. Lewis never knew her age and to this day is unsure of her real name: "She changed it to suit herself," he says. Lewis does know that her father drove a horse and cart which ferried beer, that she herself went into service as a housemaid and that she gave birth to her son two months prematurely. At that time his parents were living in an Anderson shelter in the middle of an orchard. The baby Lewis was placed in a manger ("Probably where I get my delusions of grandeur," he remarks).

It was an "untamed childhood". Together with his childhood friend Rob Earl, who would much later join Lewis as one of the original Medway Poets, he would wander the countryside from dawn til dusk. Lewis left school at fifteen with no qualifications and worked at various manual jobs, from warehouse man to apple picker to cleaner. But by his mid twenties an overwhelming desire to be an artist created an unbearable tension which resulted in a nervous breakdown.

"I see it as a good thing that turned everything around," Lewis says. After a spell in psychiatric hospital and rehabilitation and against his parents' wishes, Lewis applied for the Foundation Year at the then Medway College of Art and Design, which admitted him on the basis of a portfolio. There he met fellow artists Billy Childish and Philip Absolon, both of whom were influential.

The Medway Poets became an entity soon after Lewis left the College. Initially just Lewis and Childish, they were joined by Sexton Ming, Rob Earl and Charles Thomson. It was Lewis who christened the group – they needed a name for readings and no one could agree, possibly for the same reason that the group disbanded five years later: "There isn't a room big enough for us all to be in at the same time." They are remembered to this day.

"We actually started this whole Medway Scene," Lewis says. "We punched a hole in the wall for everything to go through – that and the fact that Billy Childish was doing his music at the same time."

I ask Lewis which he considers himself to be foremost, painter or poet. He claims poet, although admits that "sometimes when I can't say what I want to say in words, the brushes come out." His paintings are full of fantastical imagery, stunning colour and dreamlike figures. They are redolent of the works of Marc Chagall or Frieda Kahlo, with more than a touch of magic realism.

Indeed, reading Gabriel García Márquez' *One Hundred Years of Solitude* in the 80s gave his work a whole new direction. By this time he was married to Ann ("the best thing I ever did"). Together they went to Nicaragua at the height of the Civil War and a lifelong love of all things Latin American was born. Lewis spent most of the 90s touring America giving readings, leading storytelling sessions and continuing his remarkable self-education. He met and learnt from some of the leading intellectuals and literary figures of the day: among them Argentine writer Alicia Partnoy; poet and novelist Claribel Alegria, who became a life long friend and with whom Lewis performed his work both in Nicaragua and the USA; Sandy Taylor of the highly respected independent Curbstone Press and poet Carlos Rigby.

Says Lewis: "When I was thirteen I had a bad dream that I was going to die. I still believed in God then, so I said to God: 'I'm not going to die until I finish reading', so I have chain-read books ever after. From thirteen to fifty-eight I have read one book 'lit' from another, so that silly superstition helped my education."

Dovetailing with feeling burnt out by the US tours, Charles Thomson asked Lewis to join the Stuckists group at the end of the 90s. Founded by Thomson and Billy Childish, Stuckism has since become an international art movement. "At the time a lot of the Brit artists were doing things to get noticed, and we felt that was dishonest," Lewis says. "We were against art as an exercise in formalism. We believed that authenticity was more important than originality." As a Stuckist Lewis's work has been exhibited in London, Paris and Berlin.

Today the artist sides with the Remodernist movement, inclining towards a spirituality in his art. "A lot of my work is about the exile from one part of the personality from another... I think I have finally managed to make sense of my shadow. A lot of my paintings are like a magic mirror that I hold up and see something of myself in them that I didn't know about before."

I ask him if he thinks that is something that art does for artists. "It does it for artists - but if it's good enough it does it for others as well."

Emma Dewhurst

This article was originally published in *WOW Medway* magazine in September 2011

Alhambra

In this palace poised between
Water and infinity, where even
The air is covered in
      Arabic calligraphy,
A strange and mysterious
Mathematics circumvents
Logic, where seven and four do
Not equal eleven but one.
In its ceilings four is the number
By which the firmament can
Be divided and on its walls
We are told of the seven layers
Of paradise the soul must travel.
All this points to the One
From which all numbers flow.

God Is An Atheist:
She Does Not Believe In Me

God is an atheist
        She does not believe in me.
I kneel before her
        with my cross and my menorah
With psalms and sutras
        like honey on my lips
But She cannot see me;
        She is painting her mouth
With lipstick and looking
    into a compact mirror
        while wearing a blindfold.
God is an atheist
        She does not believe in me;
Beneath her throne
    an anagram, disguised
        as a dog, growls.
The moon is jealous of my tan;
The sun thinks I love someone who
Shines brighter than her.
I can no longer smell the stars,
        even on summer nights
When their blossoms
        bend close to the Earth.
God is an atheist
        She does not believe in me.
My pen ran out of poetry,
        my songs are tone deaf
And my friends and loved ones
Tear up my unwritten poems and
Scatter them over my head
        like confetti.

In The House of Ladders

In the house of ladders
A snake curls around my leg
Attempting to sink its fangs
Into the flesh of my thigh.
In the house of ladders I
Climb from level to level
Into rooms that did not exist
Until I entered them.

In the house of ladders
Some of the steps are as
Insubstantial as steam and
Dissolve beneath my shoes.
I fall Alice-like into levels
Of ill-defined, chaotic being
Where the borders of my body
Shift like the map of Europe
After the Wall came down,
And my many selves jostle
For a seat at some
Mad Hatter's tea party.

Flags

You are the flag that I raise,
The lion and the unicorn of me
With their wars of white bread
With their battles of brown bread.
My eye and my hand are the
Emblems of inner insurgencies
That foment revolution against
The tedious tyrannies of the ego.
You are the flag that I raise.
The Mogen Dovid of my once
        starless night and
The crescent moon and star
Of my thousand and one nights.
You are the flag that I raise,
The hammer and sickle of my
Immature idealism and the
Black swastika of my shadow.
You are the flag that I raise,
The red red rose of my inclination:
You are the jack of our union,
Billowing in the breeze of
Our many meetings and flying
At half mast when we part.

A Song Of Songs

My body is a song of songs
Composed of love letters
Written between an
Emerging nation and a god.

I have been badly translated
And almost airbrushed out
Of this story by scribes
And theologians who have
No place for my form in
Their schemes of control.

I awake with the dew of
Formation on my hem and
Longing pressing against
My belly like an iron weapon.

My thighs are pale antelopes
Hunted by hungry lions.
I feel a crescent moon
In my centre that resembles
A shattered glass ashtray.

Because I am blind
        you cannot see me.

The Fog Holds The House Like A Jewellery Box

The fog holds the house tight
In white gloved hands
As if it were a box of jewels.
And in a way it is,
This place that we loved
From the moment we
Crossed the doorstep.
Half of my poems were
Written here (the other
Half in cafés and bars);
Half my life I lived here
With a woman whose
Heart is so big
No poem can contain it.

The fog holds the house tight
In white gloved hands,
This brick box full
Of happy ghosts with
Its blue and white walls and
Arabic mirrors where
Strange fish swim
And angels and dark
Women hide in the
Silvered glass where
Sometimes I catch a
Split second glimpse of
　　　　　my future death.

This house lined with
Books and crammed with
Paper that must one day
Be cleared and burnt
(After I am transferred
To an even smaller box):
Letters and hoarded
Scraps, turning to ash
And throwing
Fistfuls of sparks
Into the sky, perhaps
In that garden where
Foxes courted their
Vixens and owls
Flew through my sleep.

The fog presses its
White gloved fingers
Against the window pane.
The house is adrift in
Time and space as I type
And revise and swear
At the page, cursing
Deities that I do not
Believe exist and talent
That I can only hope does.

Noughts & Crosses

He crosses the road
Like a chicken in a joke.
She crosses the tracks.
Their tracks crisscross
Constantly: at the
Level crossing; at
      the OXO gallery;
Until they zero in and
X marks the spot.
She crosses herself
Like a Catholic.
He crosses his fingers.
She crosses her eyes.
He crosses the t's
She dots the i's.
She crosses the room.
He crosses her border:
They are at a
Crossroads in their lives.
They cross the line
      of no return.
They are often at
Cross purposes.
He gets cross then
She gets cross and says:
You are the cross
That I must bear.
He double crosses her.
She triple crosses him.
She is now his ex.
And he is nothing to her.

I Wish I Were Dust On Your Shoes

I wish I were dust
        on your shoes.
I would blow
        in the air,
Fall on your flesh,
        settle on your surfaces.
I would lie like
        stockings on your
Naked legs;
            like fake tan
                on your bare arms.
I wish I were dust
                on your shoes.
I'd seep into every
        crevice of you;
Even the pores
        of your skin
    would contain
        powdered poet.

Ode To The Hand

O primordial
Abacus,
Flower of
Flesh,
Digits spread,
Petals of
Peace.
O pentagram
Of sinew
& bone,
Wearer of
Surgical
Gloves for
Entering
Mirrors
& black
Motorcycle
Gauntlets
On the
Lost highways
Of song.
O turner
Of pages
Profane &
Pornographic,
Sacred &
Serious.
O Stroker
Of cats
& dogs,
Caresser

Of tropical
Erogenous
      zones,
Of clitoral
Stutter &
Golden
Cockerel,
Of dune
& coomb,
Of knee
& swanlike
Neck &
Alabaster
Shoulder alike.
But also,
Equally,
Squeezer of
Triggers,
Signer of
      search
Warrants
      & death
Warrants
O caster of
Stones,
Stoner
Of crows &
Glass houses.
O maker of
Benedictions
& blight,
Builder of
Bridges,

Breaker of
Furniture &
Families.
O hand who
Arm wrestles
With dualisms
In the oh so
Dark
    Night of the hunter.
You giver of
Gestures,
Salutations
To statues,
Heroes &
Tyrants
(Who often
Wear the
Same face):
Remember,
O hand,
Remember this:
That open
You are
More powerful
Than closed.

In The Iron Sleep That Is Not Rest

In the iron sleep that is not rest
I drink at the bar on the corner,
An establishment that has been
Closed for years where once
They refused to serve foxes
            or gypsies with alcohol.
And I am not sure which I am,
So I leave my dark pint and
Retire to the Gents and check
            myself in the mirror
Where to my surprise I find
I am neither
            and both.

In the iron sleep that is not rest
I write letters to women who
Seem to be made of glass,
Somnambulant missives that in
The waking world they call poems.
In the iron sleep that is not rest
I dream I am a beautiful
Mad woman who fills her
House with stray typewriters
Believing them to be cats,
Never understanding why
They do not drink the endless
Saucers of milk that go sour
In every room, on every stair.

The Futurists

A mob of Modernists
Manic for movement
And Movements;
Makers of so many
Mad manifestos;

Loco over locomotion:
Railway tracks
Bursting from their
Ribs, revealing a lack
Of heart in their art.

Lusting after one
Idiot ideology
After another:
Following red flags
Liked doomed bulls,
Then falling for
Fascist falsehoods.

Hating beauty but
Making beautiful art
By default.
When I look at those
Paintings it's like
Hearing a tune I love
With lyrics I detest.

Paris

On one of those days when the city exists inside a
Blue umbrella, when the curtain of rain is drawn

Back briefly and the sky looks through at us
I'll bring to you ice from the surface of the sun.

I'll make you a set of wings like those worn by
The Peacock Angel when he visits the salty undersea

Bordello of the mermaids whose bodies glisten like
The ultramarine wet dreams of drowned sailors.

On one of those days when Paris is a city inside
A blue umbrella turned inside out by the wind

I'll sandwich you between the coffee-skinned bodies of
The two most beautiful Brazilian transsexual streetwalkers
Ever to bless the Bois de Boulogne.

I'll steal for you a fringed leather motorcycle jacket
From the sacred shoulders of Jeanne d'Arc (the one
She wears when she smokes hashish with Jim Morrison

On those wild nights in Père Lachaise).
I'll dress you in a frock fashioned from Nouvelle Vague
Film posters purchased from Scaramouche.

I'll cut my hair short like the aforementioned Joan
And sell newspapers on the street crying:
Herald Tribune! New York Herald Tribune!
And you can lure me into your stolen car.

I'll wrap you in the dark voice of Juliette Greco and
Poems purloined from the pages of Robert Desnos.

On one of those days when the city is a
Blue Umbrella turned inside out by the wind

My love will be like a yellow metro ticket or maybe
A cabbage left on the grave of Serge Gainsbourg.

Matisse

This colour is circus
And this colour
Is known as memory.

If you mix salt with light
And some fresh lemons
Straight from the tree
You get a hue
Called: Mediterranean.

It's very similar to
The Past but not quite.

This colour is Woman.
It carries a very high
Pigment load and

Is more expensive than
Any synthetic paint.

It can look to the
Untrained eye a lot
Like Mediterranean.

But there are subtle
Differences that will
Become apparent.

The Street Singer Of Montmartre

Paris has an identical twin called Buenos Aires
But they look nothing alike.

The street singer comes from Argentina
In search of KiKi, Picasso and Modigliani

But they've just left (several decades ago)
So she sings beneath the white dome

Of the sacred heart of the city of light
And tourists throw coins that turn into

Flowers, snowflakes, tears, bread and
Coffee beans as they land at her pretty feet.

She sings and KiKi, Picasso and Modigliani,
Bored by death, quit their graves and

Come to hear her sing tangos
As tourists throw coins that turn into

Rain drops and leaves that have fallen
From a lyric by another poet;

As tourists throw coins that turn into
Feathers, sequins, metro tickets and kisses,

And KiKi, Picasso and Modigliani agree
That she is one of their company

And christen her: Maria of Montmartre.

Cities

London looks for
Herself in the eyes
Of every tourist.

Paris upstages
Every actress or
Fashion model
Who makes it
Her backdrop.

Barcelona has
More curves than
All of Modernism.

Salamanca bleeds
Sunset from its
Golden walls.

Managua,
Green by default,
Has no centre but
Many hearts;
I remember
All those
          red & black valentines.

New York fills
Me up like forty
Cups of good
Strong coffee and

Shoves a paintbrush into
My impatient hand.

I Know A Girl Who Laughs In Spanish

for Maria

I know a girl who laughs in Spanish
        jajajajaja (hahahaha in English)
Sounding her J like
        we Brits sound our H.
She lives in Paris
        and has a dog called Lola
Who barks in French
        woa woa woa
                (woof woof woof in English)
Like Tintin's dog Milou
        (Snowy)
        not even guau guau guau
        like a Spanish perro.

I know a girl who laughs in Spanish
We've never met face to face
  only on Facebook;
She uses Google translation
        to talk into my heart.
Sometimes, as Madame Hergé once said
When referring to
        Captain Haddock
        ('addock in French)
I can be "such a sad English fish."
Sometimes my head spins around
        like Professor Tournesol
(Professor Calculus over here).

I know a girl who laughs in Spanish
        She is Argentine and sings the Tango.
I've never met her
but I've seen her sing on YouTube.
If she gets tired or bored with me she types
Zzzzzzzzzzzzzz
            (in Spanish or in English?)
Or if she is quiet as we chat I type
Zzzzzzzzzzzzzz:
Are they American zees
        or British zeds?
When she reads this I hope she
        jajajajas to herself.

Bird

Bird blows a
Quantum Theory
of jazz,
blows and
knows it is
the honking
of car horns
in the lost
cities of the
African Diaspora.

Bird blows
a cool cocktail
of Smokey
Sound that is
part work song
part gospel
a dash of
  (Oy Gevalt!)
Klezmer
zoot suited
and gone
in a solid way
gone (as in:
out).

Bird blows
and it goes
round and
round and
all the way

down to the
corner of
Melville and
Marquez,
meeting
at the
intersection of
Kerouac
and Poe.

Hear it blow
Hear it blow:
Hit the road
Kerouac
Don't you
Come back,
Nevermore,
Nevermore,
Nevermore.

Bird blows
and deep down
knows that
Be Bop
       breaks
the line,
the phrase
the way, in
a painting,
Georges Braque
breaks the
geometric form
of a guitar.

Bird blows
and knows
without knowing
that
Be Bop is
      Musical cubism.

US Foreign Policy In The Cold War

Eating the whirlwind.
Drinking the flame.

How come I run
Into you at all my
Best homicides?

I'm going to send you
An earthquake
Wrapped in green paper,

A little gift from your
Dutch uncle from
New Amsterdam.

I'm going to give you
A full tank of gas,

And a patina of
Tyre tracks on the
Wounded naked hills.

Little Lucy Silver Shoes

In the streets
Of Barcelona
On the mountain
Of the Jews,
I've seen you
Dance at midnight
Little Lucy
Silver shoes.
For me you're
Just a lyric,
But for real men
You are flesh.
I draw a veil
Across you
And view you
Through its mesh.
I like you in
Spanish leather
I like you in
Your dress
Of smoke.
You're so naked
With your
Clothes on,
Which you think
Is just a joke.
Sometimes you
Shine in latex,
Sometimes
In the habit

Of a nun.
Sometimes you
Bring me flowers,
Sometimes you
Bring a gun.
I'm wounded by
Your beauty
As are so many
Ugly men.
You kill me once;
You kill me twice;
And then you
Start again.

Klezmer

Clarinet goes this way,
        violin goes that way.
Double-bass goes this way,
        then that way.
They join up, then part,
        only to join
        together again.
Parting then joining
        then parting.
This is how it goes;
        this is life and
        this is music.
Make the clarinet laugh
        then cry until the
Fiddle laughs and also
        cries until they
Laugh and cry at once,
        until there is no
Difference between
        laughing and crying.
All this in the same song;
        in the same minor key?!

Rabbi

for Leonard Cohen

Like cracking eggs
          you break the hard

Shells of letters,
          releasing the sounds

They contain like a physicist
          who, through fission,

Releases the
          radiant fury of the atom.

I stand un-divided and like
          Rabbi Yeshua ben Miriam,

Hammered to history by
          the hard nails of politics.

But by these shattered
          lettershells

I am mended; by the
          brokenness of a song

So secular in its nature that
          it is holier than any hymn.

Moon Snails

Its force spent, the wave retreats,
Its reach marked by a jagged
Line of weed and foam
Dreaming of coastal erosion, of
Carnivorous tritons and diatoms,
And lichen encased in exquisite
Cell walls of fine flinty silica.
Moon snails leave their meandering
Trails on a woman's sand-coated
Belly, made sticky with
Sun screen as she whispers:
Lick my lovely bits, and he
Alliterates her with his tongue.
She looks up at the clouds until
Another wave washes across her
Golden beach
        causing her eyes to close.
It is the unchecked rip rather than
The undertow that endangers the
Bather, but as she
        lies high and dry,
Pebbles massaging her back,
The chanson of a distant shore
Is found rolled up in a castaway
Bottle of the mind, washed up and
Label-less on the long ago seashore
Of deep and azure sadness.

Night

Night in the blue attic of the fermented apple:
The Moon of Dust peeps into the skylight.
I practise the stringless acoustic guitar;
I'm almost able to get silence from
                                its sound box
            and my tarot pack has a missing card
But I don't check to see which one.
                        Some things are best not known.
The house has long since been pulled down
But the blue attic remains and I visit it
From time to time to face my fears
Which often seem identical to my desires.
Now the steep wooden steps have
                        gone and I climb through air.
The Moon of Dust wears long opera gloves
Revealing her arms and shoulders of milk.
Her dress is of flimsy clouds blown
Across her pale surface by amorous zephyrs.
Night in the blue attic of the fermented apple,
Where I wrestle with naked angels
                        and dislocate my hip in the process.
I lie panting on the floorboards,
        slick with sweat and dusted
                        with the ghosts of moths.
I take on the colour of a false dawn.
A ladder of selves extends from my head into
The starry-most heights of the firmament.

Sing To Me That I May Remember

Sing to me the song of 1000 grandmothers
   so I may know the power of
                  2000 women's arms,
   and of the strength that men are blind to:
          the love that rages without anger.
Sing to me the song of the sugar mice
   as they skitter through the
              skirting boards
   in the house of sleep and make
   their nests in the shredded
       pages of lost vanilla notebooks.
Sing to me the song that sings the singer,
   of those crowded cafes
          on rainy days in autumnal towns
  where we were once held in a
  warm coffee and tobacco scented bubble,
     rain dripping down our necks
      from steaming mackintosh collars and
  windows fogging with our breath,
     while outside the street turns to glass.
Sing to me of all these things and more
   so the blood will pass again through
     the chambers of my heart and
  I will remember, and be, just for
  the shortest while that slim gypsy poet
    you once liked so much.

Your Heart Is A Little Fist With Wings

You speak
Cartesian
Without the
Trace of
An accent.

Do not fear
The night
She is your
Twin sister.

Your heart
Is a little
Fist with
Wings that
You make
Against
The World.

And the
Tears that
You cry
Are keys
Of glass
Buried
Beneath
The doorsteps
Of exile.

Song Of The Shadow Boxer

There's no film in the camera,
The guitar's minus any strings.

This violin doesn't work,
Because it hasn't any wings.

I slept with all the bridesmaids
        at the wedding of our Lord
Then I stole his wallet and
            absconded abroad.

I played cards with coyotes;
Even forged my own name.
        I stole my own identity;
Put my anima on the game.

When I look into the mirror
With a razor in my hand

I don't trust that guy to shave me,
As I'm sure you understand.

When it comes to shadow boxing
        I really am a pro.
I've learned to love the darkness;
My favourite dish is crow.

It's Lucifer's archetype that
        illuminates the most,
Shows me my inner trinity:
Mother. Daughter. Holy Ghost.

Poem for Cristina Hoyes

Your frown is a question mark
Disguised as an exclamation

Between eyes that are slits in a
        beautiful furnace of a face.

You dance, wearing a blouse
Stained with the blood of a ghost

Between mountains of scrap metal.
Your body is an ingenious device

Translating Andalusian clichés
Into Iberian hyper-realities.

Your heel hits the ground and the
Duende rises, riding the shockwave

Of that stamp as it arches over the
Steel and satin curve of your calf,

Rippling up through a thigh that
Is the exact shape and dimension

Of an afternoon in August; stabbing
Into your sex like a dagger of sound,

Embraced by your belly, sucking
        on its sharpness.

You dance, wearing a blouse
Stained with the blood of a ghost

Among washing lines where
White bed sheets and pillow cases

Are pegged, caressed by the wind,
Like the sails of ancient armadas.

Oh Cristina who is not Carmen,
Who is more
            charismatic than Carmen.

Witched

There are apples in her voice,
A road atlas in her heart
That charts the dreadful
Strength within the land.
She picks flint arrow heads
From ploughed fields and
Feeds them to scarecrows.
She knows the sorrow of
Magpies and their secrets.
She knows the lost name of
The white horse that gallops
On our scarlet Kentish flag.

The tractor has turned over
In the top field and John,
Its driver, thinks of her black hair
Wrapped around his heart
And a Massey Ferguson on
His right leg. *He'll have a*
Limp from now on. Metal
Pins in that, for sure. Should
Have kept his furrow straight,
Says one of the men levering
The red metal monster
Off him, winking to the others
with a *know what I mean*
As they Heave Ho him free.

Greenheart

Power plant of plant power,
          greenheart of the greenwood,
Where wyrd sisters are woven
          by the web that they weave.
A weft of diversity,
          a warp of interconnectedness,
Threads that pass through us
          and connect you to me.
Power plant of plant power,
          greenheart of the greenwood,
Beating with birdlife and
          power rings of toadstools,
Amanita muscaria,
          crimson capped,
Dressed for delirium and
          also edible saffron milk cap
(lactarius deliciosus) and a
          plethora of puffballs with
          explosions of spores.
Power plant of plant power,
          ordered by the Over-mind,
Psilocybin secrets singing in
          the fungus flesh,
Where UFOnautic and numinous
          elf-machine entities turn over
New leaves that are pages in
          our almanac of seasons:
A sentient seed catalogue,
          tying nature's knots in
          the great organic internet.

Power plant of plant power,
                greenheart of the greenwood,
Larders and laboratories,
                living libraries of herb lore,
Changes, climatic and chemical,
                of solar flares and rainfall
Recorded in tree trunks
                those mandalas of history.
Power plant of plant power,
                May-flowered and may-flied,
Blue-carpeted in springtime
                like a mist of lapis lazuli,
Yet sometimes seeming
                snow-silent and star-whispered;
Roots spill from earth-banks
                Tolkeinesque and twisting
Like the tortuous tail of a
                great wurm of wisdom that
Kerns around capitals, that
                loops amongst letters in
                the hand of a scribe.
Power plant of plant power,
                you symbiotic citadel,
You church of yew trees,
                with your blackbird bibles and
Your song thrush psalms.
                An invasion of sycamore,
A stand of oak and a blaze of beech
                in fiery photosynthesis.
If we uproot you then
                we in turn are uprooted

And the Green Man wears
                   a crown of thorns
                   arms outstretched on
          a Calvary of antlers.
Power plant of plant power,
                   I underestimated your boundaries,
Thinking I'd walked in many
                   a copse, park and playing field,
Only to find I've spent
                   all my life in one forest;
                        there is no other.
The Wildwood's inside of me,
                        where Gawain went wandering
Watched by wodwoes
                        and witches,
In cottages, in clearings,
                        some made of gingerbread,
Others on chicken legs,
                        fenced in by skull posts.
Or are they just goalposts
          on the wet grass of the
Football fields of childhood?
                   I cannot tell because
                        birds must have eaten
The breadcrumb trail home.
I've travelled these places
                        as if reading a story book;
A dream book of my life.
                        Over there as a boy with
Grass-stained trouser knees,
                        khaki cap at an angle,
Bow and arrow made by my father,
                        and a sheath knife

On my belt, as I dig out
                an ammonite
From the steep wall of a
                hidden chalk quarry;
Over here on my way to
                holy Canterbury by way of
Ancient animal tracks
                skirting ley lines and the pylons
That stride like steel giants
                across the Weald,
Unchallenged by any
                passing Quixote,
Walking those pagan paths
                that we now name:
        The Pilgrim's Way.
Here I am heavenhounded
                under a cloud-berried sky
Listening to sparrow gossip
                of endless cuckoo summers.
Here I am following waterways;
                Stickleback in littlebrooks,
Blueflashed and kingfishered;
                Golden-green and dragonflied;
Minnowbright in morninglight
                with banks of wild garlic.
Power plant of plant power
                sap risen fern-friend my
Eye-thirst is unquenched;
I drink and am drunk
                on your leaf-litter laughter.
Bound by your bindweed;
                hungry for your word-hoard;
Guarded by your stag lord
                in leaf fragmented love.

Ode To The London Orbital

Bumper to bumper,
Boot to boot,
Ashes to ashes
On the M25.
Snarled up
And snarling
On the
London orbital
In our trusty
Tin snail
Of a 2CV
Listening to
Vaughan Williams'
Fantasy on
A Theme
By Thomas Tallis;
My mind's eye
Helicopters over
The countryside
Where we
Cannot drive
And only dream
Of travelling
Over wood
And tumulus,
Inner camcorder
On record mode.
O Ouroboros
Highway to
Nowhere,

This motorway is
A man made
Midgard serpent
Swallowing its own
Tar macadam tail;
We are trapped
In its coils.

Do not exceed
The 50 mile
Per hour
Speed limit.
Esso sign means
Happy motoring.
Put a tiger
In your tank.
Keep going well
Keep going Shell.
Beware the men
Of the hill fort
They have
Weapons of iron.
Tense nervous
Headache?
Paracetomol relieves
Pain instantly.
Wounded by
Elf-shot?
Send for the
Rune reader.

Tap Root

I am connected to that place,
        its dream-map I still study.
Only in memory and sleep can I visit.
        I remember a Christmas Eve
Leaving the Church porch
        after the midnight service
Back when I still believed.
        The thick voices of cattle
Complain, vapour rising
        from their nostrils
In bleak, blank fields
        pagan with frost
mirrored in the hard sparkle
        of a star strewn sky
as yet unpolluted by a misuse of neon.
        Below that stone edifice
night trains pass on the tracks;
still further below them, the river,
        like a brown snake of honey mead.
        In a drawer upstairs, I keep
A Roman coin found
        in that village I once called home.
I must have trod the mud
        that covered it because
It was found long after I left
        by a man with a metal detector.
A Roman coin dropped
      perhaps a few centuries after Christ
      by the owner of the villa
whose stones augment the corner
      of that 12th century place of worship.

A Roman coin that connects me
                    with that night
and all the brittle glittering nights of
                    my youth.

Lynx Legends

Based on Innu and Siberian myths

Eating winter makes your mouth cold
Says the Canadian lynx as he measures
The thighs of his new human wife.
He keeps marrying them for love
But the food has a habit of running
Out halfway through that dark and
Desolate season and their legs end up
On that big roasting stick of his.

Eating winter makes your mouth cold
Says the Siberian lynx, fixed to a
Tree in the far north by a gold chain.
When she walks sun-wise
                she tells stories;
When she walks widdershins she
                recites poetry.
Pushkin once sat at her feet taking
Dictation and translating from cat into
                Cyrillic script.
Her yellow eyes burn like ice.

Eating winter makes your mouth cold
Says the Canadian lynx, salivating.
He lifts up my white doe skin dress and
Takes out his retractable tape measure.

If this goes on, I say shivering, *you do
Know that the matrimonial agency will
Refuse to send you any more clients?*
I can never tell if he's making love

(58)

To me or if he's just raiding the ice box.
But the larder will soon be bare and
His roasting stick is so terribly sharp.

A Poet On Fire

Cast out, I fall like a meteor
burning up in your atmosphere,
scratching the dark sky
like an engraver's tool
       on a copper plate.
Cast out like
       a troublemaking angel
who sometimes has
       the face of a felonious fox;
Cast out, I fall into you,
with a notebook full of stolen
       fire and reflected beauty;
I fall and fall into your flesh
  and write poems
       beneath your skin.

Dream Jobs

In the dream I tried
To dial your number
But had no control
Over the digits,
And the hospital
That I worked in
Thirty years ago
Was also the supermarket
I worked in
Forty years ago.

I spent the morning
Sterilising medical
Instruments and
Stacking cans of
Baked beans into
Promotional pyramids.
In the afternoon I
Sent suture sets and
Vaginal speculums to
The Butchery Department
And Fresh Fish counter.

In both jobs I wore a
White coat, so at least
That was not confusing.

And still I tried
To dial your number,
But got instead
Strange voices telling

Me weather forecasts
And cryptic messages
Like those sent to the
French Resistance
Or from Death's car radio
In Cocteau's Orphée.

They let me go home
Early from both jobs
As it was Christmas Eve,
But already the shops
Were closing and
I had not bought any
Gifts or food for the
Holiday because it
Was July when I
Clocked on this morning.

In The Language of Nightingales

In the language of
Nightingales,
In the dark and
Dusty trees
Above the nocturnal
Railway station

I hear thoughts that
I imagined were
Only in my head
Until now, turned
Into songs, that
Are un-writeable.

The Great Bear
Burns in the black
Above the cement
Loaf of a doorstep.
The house is asleep
And I am halfway
To joining it.

Tonight I will
Dream of shadows
Chasing each other
Across a sun dial
In a walled garden
Where it is always
Midnight and I
Am wearing a blue
Dress stolen from
God's wardrobe.

There is a postcard
In my breast pocket
Postmarked: The Past,
A country I once
Visited although I
Could not stay long.

On it is written
A poem that I can't read
Because it is in
French or Spanish
Or perhaps even
In the language of nightingales.

They all sound so similar
When I am asleep.

The Algebra Of My Sadness

Like a dream, a poem is its
Own meaning. If it could be
Said any other way
It would have;
    but it couldn't;
        and it wasn't.
It's like trying to tell you
The colour of triangles,
Or the sound a circle makes
When you hold it in your eye.
It's as if you want me to
Tell you the square root
Of blue, or the exact number
Of red; or to compare the
Shape of love when seen
From far off to the same
Shape seen from within;
Or the algebra of my sadness
When you walk away from me
Having forgotten to wave;
   or worse still, not
     waved having
       not forgotten.
Let the psychologists explain
The fairytales and
Let the theologians
Explain the parables.
There's always a detail
That cannot be explained
Beyond prose and reason.
That is what poetry is for.

If it could have been said
Any other way
   it would have;
      but it couldn't;
         and it wasn't.

My Dress Is On Fire

My dress is on fire,
                it blazes like summer
    no matter what
                time of year it actually is.
Peach coloured,
           floral prints
on a blinding white background.

My dress is on fire,
                it fits me like a rumour,
   caresses when I walk,
       floats on my surface
                like oil on water.
I am more naked wearing
        it than when I am nude.

My dress is on fire,
                it absorbs my heat,
   my body is the sun
          beneath the earth
(Minerva Sulis).

My dress is on fire,
               I am one with it
In the bleached brightness
               of the noon;
That little midnight
               of the morning,
When the eternal choirs
               of cicadas pause,
Just for a moment,
               and start again,
Their song's direction changed.

My dress is on fire,
    it is part of
My molten form:
               my mercurial nature
displayed on the outside of me.

The Sun Is A Yellow Dog Holding A Blue Bone In Its Mouth

The sun is a yellow dog holding a blue poem in its mouth like a bone.

Oh happy sun, so pleased with the juicy day.

In a town that should have been a city (had the local council filled in the paperwork on time) a man sits at a pavement café near the ancient Cathedral and scribbles in his notebook as the Cathedral bells ring out the hour.

Across the street another man enters a phone box and calls a woman. He tells her how blue the sky is, although all she has to do is look out of the window and see for herself.

The man at the café counts the syllables in the lines he has written.

There are nineteen syllables.

He crosses out: *like a bone.* He frowns, now there are sixteen.

The other man finishes his call and leaves the phone box, still holding the woman's voice as if it were a bunch of flowers.

The man at the café ignores the flowers as they have far too many syllables.

He changes the *a* to *an* and the *blue* to *azure.*

Now the poem is technically better but he so loved the simplicity of the blue and hates the fussiness of the azure.

Despite the sun he is frowning.

In the sky the yellow dog yawns and lets go of the blue bone.

The man at the café watches his whole day plummet to earth.

At that same moment, the other man who holds the woman's voice as if it were a bunch of flowers looks up and sees not an azure bone but a blue balloon floating free from the jaws of the sun.

What a day, he thinks, what a wonderful day.

The man at the café notices the man who is holding the woman's voice as if it were a bunch of flowers, looking up at the sky and smiling like an idiot.

He returns to the page and writes:

One man's wonderful day is another man's unsuccessful haiku.

Then he begins to count the syllables in the sentence he has just written and he begins to smile.

By some mystery the sentence, like a cat caught in a physicist's thought experiment, becomes both true and untrue at the same time.

Recipe

Take a fresh alarm clock
Break it into a blue bowl
With white stripes on it
(if you don't have one you
can use a white bowl
with blue stripes instead).

Beat the mixture into the
Consistency of a thin batter.
Add Time and Seasons.
Place the mixture in the fridge
(Gas Mark 6) for three days.
On the third day it will rise
And ascend to heaven.

Meanwhile, take a bag of
Nuts from the cupboard.
Read the instructions on
The back of the packet.
When you get to the bit
That says: WARNING this
Product may contain
Traces of nuts, you can

Smile or grimace
And make a remark out loud
About the litigious nature
Of our modern society.
Realising you are alone
And feeling foolish, put the
Nuts back in the cupboard,

As this recipe does
Not require them.

Return to the fridge.
On opening it and finding it
Empty consider starting a
New religion but change your
Mind quickly because you
Are very hungry.

Take the mixture into the
Dining room and remember:
You are a dish that
Must be consumed hot.

Wear Me

Wear me
Like a fever.
Wear me
Like a garment
Without seams;
A dress made
Of perspiration.
Press yourself
Into my
Softest places
Until my
Body changes
Its scent
And takes
On the aroma
Of chestnut trees
In the rain
In the pale
Autumnal city
Of your broken sleep.

I Will Always Remember The Words You Did Not say

I will always remember
The words you did
        not say.
Teeth teeter on
Opening, then faulter,
Remaining closed:
The moment is lost.
The retort rescinds,
The outburst dammed up,
Its waters calmed.
Sometimes for the best
But not always so.
I will always remember
The words you did
        not say.
Also those I did not answer.
In time those words come
Back to haunt us, as much
If not more so than
Those that actually were.

Poem To My Never Born Children

In an eternal waiting room sit my unfathered children.
They read my unpublished and unwritten works
Wondering to themselves why I preferred
                              these words to them.
I want them to know that yes, I would have
Loved them, but I feared that I would have been like
                              My weak father and my selfish mother.
If I had been as good a person as I am a poet
Then I would have flown kites with them on windy days
Upon the Great Lines of Chatham, and told them such
Stories of ravens who stole the sun and moon and stars,
Of foxes that tricked the Angel of Death and of
Golden haired girls arrested for breaking and entering
                              the property of bears.
In an eternal waiting room my unfathered children
Sit reading and waiting, never being told: NEXT.

Black Honey

Sword of honey,
Furnace-fashioned by
Blacksmith bees on
An anvil of flowers.

Sword of honey,
Black honey of
The merciless eye
        of summer,
Evaporating saliva
From the mouth of
The exhausted afternoon.

Sword of honey,
Stiff and sticky
With amber light,
Penetrating the petals
Of seconds and
Minutes and the
Labyrinthine chambers
Of the golden hours.

The darkness of summer
Is the brightest black,
Fiery corona of the
Total eclipse burning
Out the optic nerve,
Burning out the
        light bulb of ideas.

A rune scratched into
The red darkness on the
Inside of your eyelid.

Do They Also Praise You In The Darkness Without Cease?

Do they also sing your name
In the darkness without cease?
Do they praise it in the vast
Expanse between galaxies,
Against the pulsar's pulse
And background radiation
Left over from the Big Bang,
And the crushing pull of the
White Dwarf, and beyond the
Event horizon of the Black Hole?
Do they praise you from
Infinite hives or from the
Suspended animation chambers
Lost in the light years between
This star or that star or another?
Do they also sing your name with
Beaks or mouths that move from
Left to right not up and down
With clicks and whirrs and
Strange metallic sounds that
Scrape and buzz, alien to the
Vocal cords of primates?
And this name that they praise,
As they raise tentacles or perhaps
Arms beyond counting,
Is it the one that we also praise?
Or is it as I suspect with
Different letters and other
Sounds alien to our ears?
Does that make it
                less holy, or more?

When He Has Gone

When he has gone,
His voice caresses her
Again and again
From the answerphone.
When he has gone,
She wears his smell
Against her skin like an
Invisible nightdress;
Delaying her shower
For as long as possible.
When he has gone,
His spent desire
Lies on her belly like
A strand of pearls.
When he has gone,
She holds his
Shadow between her legs;
And still the other side
Of the bed
Is a frost covered field.

Beneath The Big Sky

They put a sea between us
But our words were paper boats.

They grew a forest between us
But our words cut a path.

They put mountains between us
But our words could climb.

They put prose between us
But our words were poetry.

That sky above your head is
The same sky above mine.

The Last Poem

You have these dreams where you find a door in
our house that was not there before. You open it
and find a room you've never noticed until now,
despite living here for the last thirty years. I know
you have these dreams because you've told me
about them. Sometimes the room is full of ornate
furnishings, sometimes treasure. Well, when I'm
gone, that is where you'll find me. There, and
only there, in that room behind your eyes. If, by
some chance, I'm not there (I may be visiting
dead friends), in that room on a table there will be
a poem. I'll put it in an envelope and write your
name on it so that you will be sure that it is for
you. Please read it. When you do read it you'll
wonder, typically, the name of the beautiful woman
who inspired it, never guessing it was you. I say
this because I know you so well. Read it again
carefully and remember how I always looked at
you and how you could see what you really looked
like in the mirror of my eyes.

Bloody Foxes

A fox tried to enter my latest poem.
I told him to go away: I already have

Far too many of his species in my work.
People will think I'm trying to be
A second rate Ted Hughes.

The fox was a bit put out by this and told
Me so in no uncertain terms: "You also
Have angels and women and guitars, I
Don't hear you telling any of them to leave."

He is right of course: foxes usually are.
"And besides" he added,
"I'm already here."

I'm stuck with foxes it seems: in my
Garden; on my doorstep at 4am on a
Winter morning when I trip over one,
Thinking it is my neighbour's cat.

Stuck with foxes in the Medway Towns
As they walk down Glencoe Road
At noon as if they owned the place,
Watching me, heads cocked,
As I photograph my paintings;
As I sing or talk to myself.

I'm stuck with foxes:
In my poems; in my stories; in my dreams.
"Oh stay then," I sigh.

I realise that
It is not me, never me, who decides.
My pointy faced friend
                    has pointed this out.
Even the point of this poem is not mine.